DINOSAURS
OF THE LAND, SEA AND AIR

by Michael Teitelbaum

THE FACTS ABOUT DINOSAURS

The Rourke Corporation, Inc.
Vero Beach, FL 32964

Library of Congress Cataloging-in-Publication Data
Teitelbaum, Michael.
    Dinosaurs of the land, sea and air / by Michael Teitelbaum.
       p. cm. — (The Facts about dinosaurs)
    ISBN 0-86593-353-7
    1. Dinosaurs—Juvenile literature. [1. Dinosaurs.] I. Title. II. Series.
QE862.D5T43   1994
567.9'1—dc20
                                          93-49614
                                            CIP

Printed in the USA
                                           AC

CONTENTS

VELOCIRAPTOR
(veh-loss-ih-RAP-tor)

Velociraptor means "swift plunderer." It was a small, meat-eating dinosaur. As its name tells you, Velociraptor was able to run very fast. It was lightly built and very agile. This helped it track down its **prey**, even in the dense forest.

Velociraptor was a deadly hunter. Often it would hunt in packs. While one Velociraptor would charge straight at the victim, others would attack from the sides. Whichever way the prey turned, it was trapped.

Velociraptor had a long, low head and a flat skull. It had long fingers. Each finger contained a razor-sharp claw. Each of its feet had four toes. One of its toes was a large, hook-like claw. This claw was its most lethal weapon.

*A member of the **Coelurosaur** family of dinosaurs, Velociraptor could attack while standing on one leg, using its tail for balance.*

4

ARCHAEOPTERYX
(ar-kee-OP-ter-ix)

Many scientists believe that Archaeopteryx was the world's first bird. Some think that it was the link between land dinosaurs and real birds. Archaeopteryx's name means "ancient feathers." It is the earliest known animal to have feathers.

Its feathers probably developed from the **evolution** of the creature's **reptile** scales. The scales split open and trapped air, allowing Archaeopteryx to fly. Its feathers also helped it to keep warm in the cool night air.

Archaeopteryx was about three feet long, and its skinny body weighed about 20 pounds. Unlike birds, which have no teeth, this winged animal had small teeth. Archaeopteryx ate mostly insects, which it trapped in its feathered wings.

Although it could fly, Archaeopteryx did not fly very well. It fluttered around just above the ground, the way chickens do.

PLESIOSAURUS
(PLEE-zee-uh-sawr-us)

Plesiosaurus was a fish-eating **marine** reptile. It propelled itself through **prehistoric** waters with powerful, paddle-shaped flippers. Although it lived in the water, it laid its eggs on land.

Plesiosaurus had a long, snake-like neck, a barrel-shaped body, and a small head. It swam close to the surface of the oceans it inhabited and used its long neck to search for food below the surface.

Plesiosaurus evolved from an earlier group of sea reptiles called **Nothosaurs**. Nothosaurs had lizard-like bodies, long necks, and jagged teeth. They had webbed feet and a fin on their tails. As Plesiosaurus developed, its head got smaller, and its neck got longer. Its limbs became powerful paddles, which helped to make Plesiosaurus an excellent swimmer.

*A **paleontologist** once described Plesiosaurus as a large snake threaded through the body of a turtle.*

8

CHASMOSAURUS
(KAZ-muh-sawr-us)

Chasmosaurus was a member of the **Ceratopsian** family of dinosaurs. It had two horns on its head and another horn growing out of its **snout**. Chasmosaurus also had a large bony frill. But unlike some of its relatives, Chasmosaurus's frill had holes in it.

The holes made the enormous bony plate lighter than that of a dinosaur like Triceratops, so it was easier for Chasmosaurus to move its large head around. The light frill also helped it to run faster than its bulkier Ceratopsian cousins.

This parrot-beaked plant-eater grew to a size of 17 feet in length. It weighed from three to five tons. Chasmosaurus had strong neck muscles. It needed these to pull out the roots of tough plants, which it loved to eat.

Although Chasmosaurus was as large as a rhinoceros, it could run as fast as a horse.

PTERANODON
(tair-AN-o-don)

Pteranodon weighed only 33 pounds. It had a turkey-sized body. On its head sat a **crest** that was six feet long. Pteranodon had a long, toothless beak and ate mostly fish.

Pteranodon was actually not a dinosaur. It belonged to a family of flying reptiles called **Pterosaurs**. Although Pteranodon had a wingspan of 27 feet, it could only have flown in light wind. It was probably a glider rather than a true bird-like flyer.

There are many theories about the purpose of Pteranodon's long crest. It may have been used as a brake for landing from a flight. It may have been used to steer Pteranodon during flight. Or the crest may simply have acted as a balance for the creature's long beak.

Unlike a dinosaur, Pteranodon was warm-blooded and may have actually had fur.

12

HYPSILOPHODON
(hip-sih-LO-fuh-don)

Hypsilophodon was a very small dinosaur. It was only four or five feet long, and weighed only 130 pounds. It was no bigger than a large dog. It had a six-inch head and very large eyes, so it could easily spot the big meat-eating dinosaurs that might attack it.

Hypsilophodon was part of a family of two-legged, plant-eating dinosaurs called **Ornithopods**. They were grazing animals, who, much like deer today, munched on **cycads**. Hypsilophodon was also one of the fastest dinosaurs ever. It ran on two legs, using its tail for balance.

Hypsilophodon may have been the only plant-eater that could outrun the smaller, meat-eating dinosaurs of its time.

Speedy Hypsilophodon ran on its toes, the same way birds do today.

14

APATOSAURUS
(ah-PAT-uh-sawr-us)

This dinosaur was originally called Brontosaurus (BRON-tuh-sawr-us), which means "thunder lizard." It got this name because it shook the earth when it walked. This huge creature was 70 feet long and weighed over 30 tons.

Apatosaurus was a member of the group of gentle, plant-eating dinosaurs called **Sauropods**. It had a very long neck that measured 20 feet from head to shoulders. This long neck helped Apatosaurus reach leaves in tall trees. It had small teeth that were shaped like pegs. Apatosaurus spent a long time chewing its food, and ate as much as 1,000 pounds of leaves a day.

At one time paleontologists believed that Apatosaurus was stupid. They now believe that these gentle giants were fairly intelligent creatures.

Apatosauruses travelled in herds, keeping their young in the center of the herd to protect them from attack.

16

IGUANODON
(ig-WAN-oh-don)

Iguanodon means "iguana tooth." It got its name because it had teeth like those of today's iguana lizard, only much bigger. Iguanodon weighed about five tons, about the size of an elephant, but it looked more like a chubby, overgrown kangaroo.

This **herbivore** usually searched for food on all four legs. When it ran, Iguanodon used its powerful back legs. It also stretched up on these back legs to reach high leaves on trees.

Iguanodon could wrap its tongue around reeds and thick grasses and pull them into its mouth. Small branches and tough roots were crunched with its two rows of grinding teeth, located in its cheeks.

Iguanodon had a sharp spike on each of the thumbs of its front legs, which it used to fight off meat-eating attackers.

18

ICHTHYOSAURUS
(ik-thee-uh-SAWR-us)

Ichthyosaurus was not a dinosaur. It was a fish-eating marine reptile. Its name means "fish lizard." It looked very much like a shark, dolphin, or swordfish. It had a long pointed nose, a narrow head, and many tiny, razor-sharp teeth.

This excellent swimmer also had two pair of flippers, a fin on its back, and a fish-like tail. Ichthyosaurus was 33 feet long, and it spent its time swimming in the ocean, hunting for fish.

Although it looked like a fish and swam in the sea, Ichthyosaurus was an air-breathing animal. It never left the water, but it often had to come to the surface to take in a fresh supply of air, much like a whale or dolphin does today.

Ichthyosaurus kept her eggs in her body until they hatched, then gave birth to live babies.

20

TRICERATOPS
(try-SAIR-uh-tops)

This three-horned dinosaur had a bony plate on its head. The plate and horns protected it from damaging attacks. Its mouth looked like the beak of a parrot. Scientists know a great deal about this dinosaur. In 1900, more than 30 Triceratops skulls were found at one time in Wyoming.

Scientists once believed that this four-legged herbivore was a slow creature. Today it is thought that Triceratops moved like a modern day rhinoceros. It may have been able to gallop at a fairly high speed. It is also believed that Triceratops were **aquatic** dinosaurs.

Triceratops ate plants with very tough leaves. It could do this because of special sharp teeth that crushed and sliced its food.

Triceratops's bony head plate was six feet long— the size of a tall person.

22

GLOSSARY

Aquatic—Living in or near a body of water, such as a lake or ocean.

Ceratopsian—A group of plant-eating dinosaurs that had horns or frills on their heads.

Coelurosaurs—Small meat-eating dinosaurs that were vicious killers.

Crest—A crown-like piece of bone that stuck out of the back of the head of some dinosaurs.

Cycads—Tough, primitive, tropical plants, resembling palms.

Evolution—The development of an animal or species. As a species evolves, its characteristics change.

Herbivore—A plant-eating animal.

Marine—Living in the sea.

Nothosaurs—An early group of sea reptiles with lizard-like bodies, long necks, and jagged teeth.

Ornithopods—A group of swift, two-legged, plant-eating dinosaurs.

Paleontologist—A scientist who studies dinosaurs.

Prehistoric—Relating to a period of time before recorded history.

Prey—The victim of a meat-eating animal.

Pterosaurs—Flying reptiles that lived at the same time as the dinosaurs.

Reptile—A cold-blooded, egg-laying animal that crawls on its belly or walks on short legs.

Sauropods—Four-legged, plant-eating dinosaurs. They weighed up to 80 tons and were the biggest of all the dinosaurs.

Snout—The nose and jaws of an animal.